FESTIVAL

of

LIGHTS

Feast of Dedication: Hanukkah

CHELSEA KONG

AuthorHouse™
1663 Liberty Drive
Bloomington, IN 47403
www.authorhouse.com
Phone: 833-262-8899

This book is printed on acid-free paper.

ISBN: 978-1-6655-4090-2 (sc)
ISBN: 978-1-6655-4091-9 (e)

Print information available on the last page.

Published by AuthorHouse 10/12/2021

authorHOUSE®

Festival of Lights

Feast of Dedication

Temple photo (photo by the Author)

The feast is also called Hanukkah, which Jewish children celebrate instead of Christmas to remind them about the Dedication of the Temple.

What Is the Festival of Lights?

The Festival of Lights begins on Kislev 25 and is eight days long.

In the Western calendar, it falls in November or December.

The word *Hanukkah* means "dedication" and is related to lights.

It's celebrated around the same time as Christmas to mark the rededication of the Temple in 165 B.C.

A happy Hanukkah scene with menorah, doughnut, dreidel, and gelt

What God Word Says

The time came for the Feast of Dedication at Jerusalem. This was during the winter. Jesus was walking in the Temple in Solomon's Porch. (John 10:22-23)

God will shake the nations and fill the temple with His glory (Haggai 2:7).

God said that He will make the later Temple greater than the past one (Haggai 2:9).

Temple of Solomon

Why Celebrate?

The celebration reminds God's people of the Temple of God.

It reminds them of the dark times when they were being chased by their enemies.

God wanted His people to remember Him.

It points to Jesus who makes us clean by His blood. He is the Light of the World.

Entrance to the Temple of Solomon

When Does It Start?

Hanukkah begins on the eve of Kislev 25 in the Jewish calendar, often about the same time as December 23.

Kislev can occur anywhere from late November to late December.

We need to check the calendar to know the dates.

The Jewish calendar gives more details.

2021 calendar

Celebration for Eight Days

Women are to stop the housework every evening.

They are to light the lights each night.

Women light the Hanukkah menorah (lampstand) because they are part of the miracle.

It became a holiday in the dark times.

Children get gifts.

Woman lighting a candle

Menorah

The menorah is the candlestand used for lighting the candles.

It has nine candles on it. One candle is used to light the other candles from left to right. This candle also sits taller than the others.

It reminds us of Jesus Christ, who gives us light.

A blessing is said when lighting the candle each night.

Colorful Hanukkah in the dark

Blessing 1

The first blessing spoken is:

Baruch atah Adonai, Eloheinu melech haolam, asher kid'shanu b'mitzvotav v'tsivanu l'hadlik ner shel Hanukkah.

(Blessed are You, Adonai our God, Ruler of the Universe, who makes us holy with your commandments, commanding us to kindle [light] the Hanukkah lights.)

Menorah with four candles lit and doughnut

Blessing 2: Miracles

The second blessing spoken is:

Baruch atah Adonai, Eloheinu melech haolam, she-asah nisim laavoteinu v'imoteinu bayamim hahaeim baz'man hazeh.

(Blessed are You, Adonai our God, Ruler of the Universe, who performed wondrous deeds for our ancestors in those ancient days at this season.)

Girl looking at sky with big moon at night

Blessing 3: First Night of Hanukkah Prayer)

The third blessing spoken is:

Baruch atah Adonai, Eloheinu melech haolam, shehecheya-nu v'kiy'manu v'higiyanu laz'man hazeh.

(Blessed are You, Adonai our God, Ruler of the Universe, who has kept us alive, sustained us, and brought us to this season.)

The menorah is put in the front window for everyone to see.

**A woman lights the menorah with a candle, using
one hand, with a doughnut on the table**

Sing Songs

Songs are sung on Hanukkah.

It's good to sing a new song to the Lord.

It is a great time to sing praises to Him.

A girl sings Hanukkah songs into a microphone

Dreidel Game

Children play a game of dreidel, is a spinning top.

The game originates in ancient Greece and Rome.

Children come together and get gelt and chocolate coins for poker chips.

They take turns spinning the dreidel to win or get nothing.

A big dreidel

Dreidel Words

Each time they spin, the dreidel will create words.

It tells about the Hanukkah story.

A great miracle happened there.

Children can win half a pot or lose some gelt.

Candles, dreidel, and gelt

Food

There are traditional foods made with oil.

It is the time of the miracle of the oil.

There are foods made with cheese.

Doughnut on a gold plate, dreidels, and gelt in the background

Cheese Latkes and Sauces

Among the foods are cheese latkes, as well as potato latkes cooked in oil.

There is sour cream and applesauce.

Potato pancakes

Braided Egg Bread

There is one bread called *challah* that Jews eat to celebrate.

It is sweet and made with sugar.

It is eaten with cheese.

Challah braided bread

Doughnuts

Jews also eat *sufganiyot*, or doughnuts fried in oil.

There are also the smaller doughnuts that look like balls.

Doughnuts

Other Items

There is also a bottle of wine and a bottle of oil, along with parched corn, dry figs, bread, and cheese.

Dried figs

John 10:22–25

Jesus was walking in the Temple of Solomon.

The people wanted to know if He was the Messiah.

He told them that they must believe in the Father.

Believe in God's Words.

Solomon's Temple

Jesus the Messiah

Jesus is the Messiah that God promised.

He died on the cross for all the sins of the world.

It is by His blood that we are clean from sin.

He gave us a new life to dedicate to God.

Jesus carries the cross

Jesus, the Light of the World

Jesus is the Light that Father God gave to the world.

He makes us understand His Word and may let us see the unseen things.

His light shines without limit and never ends.

It is during this festival that Jesus told the people He is the Bread of Life, and His Blood is given to us to bring us to the Father.

Hanukkah, sitting in the dark with blue curtain

Salvation Prayer

God, I know that I have sinned against you. Forgive me for the wrong that I have done. I believe that Jesus Christ died on the cross for me and that He rose from the grave after three days—that I can have His long-lasting life. Come into my heart to be my Lord and Savior. I choose to turn away from the wrong I did and choose to follow you. Lead me to walk with you. Keep me safe and teach me your ways. Stop every bad thing in my life that has an open door to hurt me. Close those doors. Holy Spirit, fill me now in Jesus's name. Amen.

Asian girl praying with head down on Bible

Baptism in the Holy Spirit

Jesus, you are the one that fills me with Your Spirit. Come, Holy Spirit, and come into my life and fill me to overflow with Your presence. Come with your fire too. Thank you for the gift of tongues in Jesus's name. Amen.

Open your mouth and let the words come out that God gives you. It will be words that you don't know the meaning of. God can give you the meaning when you ask Him. Keep giving God your mouth to speak it out. You need to let Him talk through you every day to grow this gift. He will also take you closer to God, and you will know more about Jesus and have power from God to do great things and know things.

Dove

Prayer

Father God, remind me of what Jesus has done. I dedicate my life to Jesus. Thank you for saving me. Thank you for Your light that breaks the darkness. Thank you that You are the Savior of the world. Thank you for protection in Jesus' name. Amen.

Praying at the West Wall (photo by the Author)

Message from the Author

The Temple was dedicated to the Lord, both the first time when Solomon made it and when it was built again. Jesus wants us to rededicate to Him. He wants us to remember He is the light. He is the one that saved us from evil. He gave us the everlasting life. He is the miracle that happened.

Child with Hanukkah cards

References

"Chanukkah Candle Lighting Blessings." Judaism 101, 1998-2021, https://www.jewfaq.org/chanukahref.htm.

Nykiel, Teddy. "Your Guide to 7 Traditional Hanukkah Foods." *Taste of Home*, 2021, https://www.tasteofhome.com/article/traditional-hanukkah-foods.

Other Products

The Bridal Collection
Knowing God
How to Hear God's Voice
New Life in Jesus
Loving Israel
God's Gifts
Meeting God
Word Power
Fruit of the Spirit
The Tabernacle
Bride for Jesus
A Life of Prayer
Live Free
Who am I in Jesus
Walk in Love
God's Favor
Man of God
Woman of God
How to Use Money
God's Wisdom
Fasting
See Jerusalem and Bethany
First Fruit Offering
Pentecost
Feast of Trumpets
Day of Atonement
Feast of Tabernacles
Counting the Omer
Festival of Lights
Glory, Presence, and Holy Spirit
Live in God's Presence

31 Day Devotional
Biblical Puzzle Book Vol 1
Biblical Puzzle Book Vol 2
Biblical Puzzle Book Vol 3
Biblical Puzzle Book Vol 4
Biblical Puzzle Book Vol 5
Bible Puzzles for Young Children Book 1
Bible Puzzles for Young Children Book 2
Bible Puzzles for Young Children Book 3
Biblical Puzzle Book for Children Book 1
Biblical Puzzle Book for Children Book 2
Biblical Puzzle Book for Children Book 3

Teaching Series & Guides
How to Hear God's Voice Teaching Guide
Knowing God, Jesus, and Holy Spirit: Children Guide Book
Relationship with God, Jesus, Holy Spirit Guide

Teaching (Non-Sale)
Purim
Passover
Resurrection

and much more!

Please check Chelsea's website for links to other books and products found on Amazon, Barnes & Noble, and Kobo. Please leave a review to help the author to write more books. Thank you!

https://chelseak532002550.wordpress.com
YouTube: https://www.youtube.com/channel/UCOvw9wUmkE08Akeq2z3TQVA

Printed in the United States
by Baker & Taylor Publisher Services